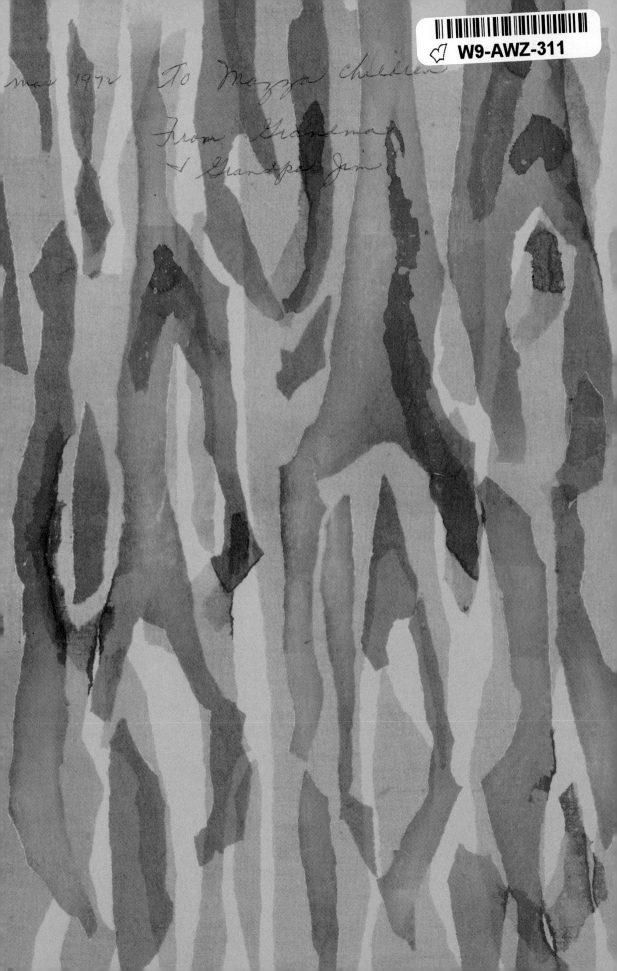

Mar 1972   To Mezzal children

         From Grandma
         & Grandpa Jim

W9-AWZ-311

A WORLD IN A TREE

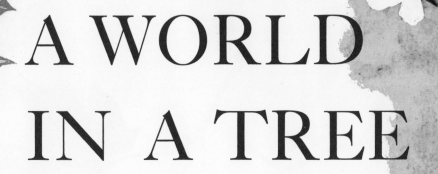

A WORLD
IN A TREE

Written by

STANLEY KLEIN

Illustrated by

MARIAN MORTON

Doubleday & Company, Inc.
Garden City, New York

LIBRARY OF CONGRESS CATALOG CARD NUMBER 67–19131
COPYRIGHT © 1968 BY DOUBLEDAY & COMPANY, INC.
ALL RIGHTS RESERVED
PRINTED IN THE UNITED STATES OF AMERICA
FIRST EDITION

Winter. The snow falls. A chilling wind blows and whips each falling snowflake into a strange and silent dance. Amid this white and peaceful world stands a tall, almost bare, maple tree. The tree seems lifeless. It looks as if it were a skeleton whose only purpose is to remind the world that life once existed here.

But things are not always as they appear. The seemingly lifeless skeleton of the tree is not lifeless. Nor is the silent world of the tree really silent and inactive. Above, below, and all around the tree, life goes on. And as winter turns to spring, spring to summer, and summer to fall, the tall maple will become the center of an exciting world—the world of a tree.

WINTER

Winter in the Northeast. The activity of fall is over. The leaves of the maple lie buried beneath a blanket of white sparkling snow. The roots of the tree no longer remove water and minerals from the frozen ground. The tree will not grow until spring returns.

For many animals, winter is also a time of rest. They no longer move about leading active lives. Some may even be hard to find or recognize—but they have not disappeared. Hidden in the cracks of the tree bark or buried under the fallen leaves are insects, such as mosquitoes, wasps, queen bees, and beetles. And small silky cocoons of spider eggs seem to hug the bare twigs or fill the small crevices in the bark. Nearby, black carpenter ants have hollowed out a shelter in a fallen limb. Almost every crevice serves as a home for some living creature.

And dangling high on a wavering twig are several tightly rolled leaves. Inside these shelters, or chrysalids, other insects are passing through an early stage of life. When warm weather returns they will emerge as viceroy butterflies.

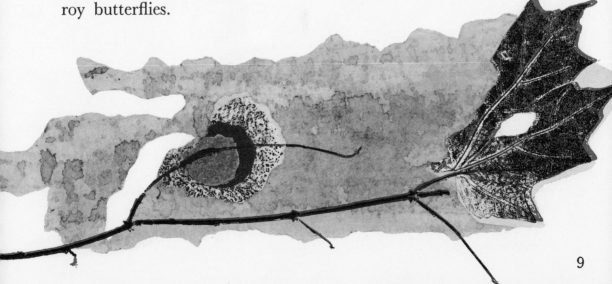

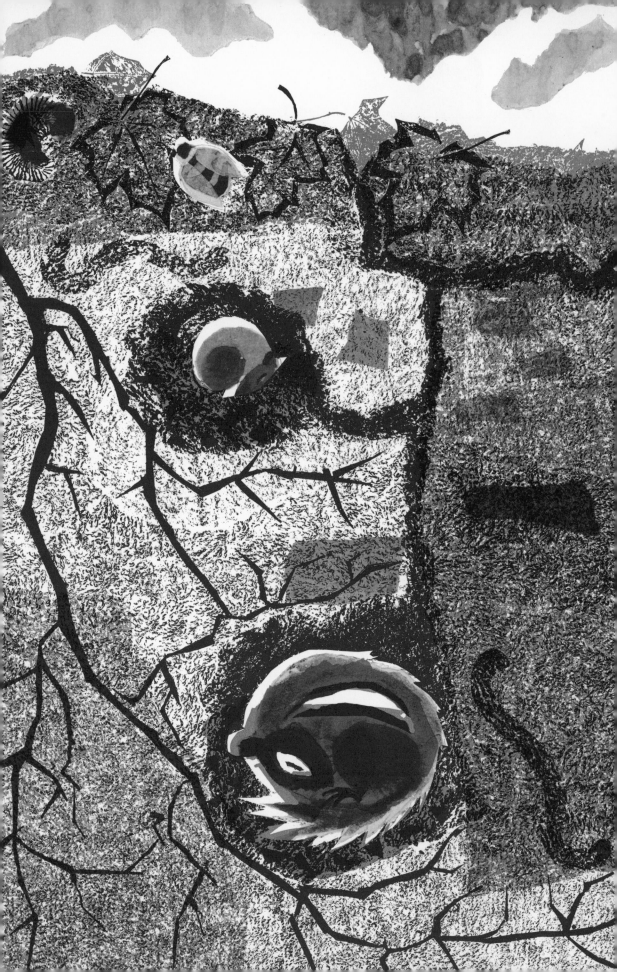

Under the ground, beneath the white snow and tangled roots, other animals rest and are protected from the cold. Buried in the layer of leaves dropped from the maple are other bees, wasps, and slugs. Here too lies the earthworm—motionless, unable to burrow through the frozen ground.

Curled up tightly nearby is the brown- and black-banded woolly bear. This grizzly-haired little caterpillar is also passing through an early stage of life on its way to adulthood. Several months from now the woolly bear will be hard to recognize as it flutters off as a delicate white moth.

Sometimes a field mouse in his grayish winter coat can be seen darting across the snow searching for food. But more often he too is at rest, burrowed in a warm shelter beneath the snow-covered surface.

And perhaps most peaceful of all is the chipmunk. Hibernating two or three feet below ground, he may sleep a day, a week, or even many weeks while the biting cold of winter passes.

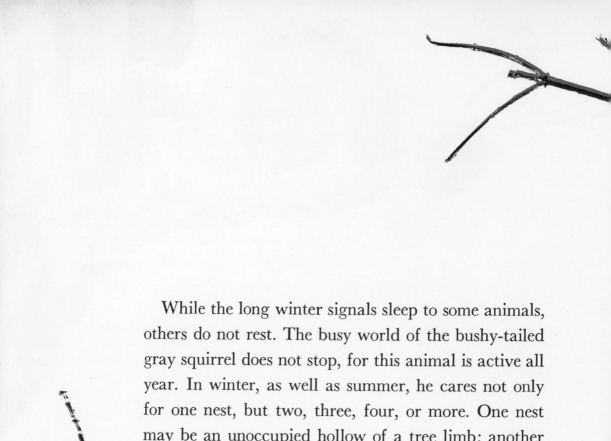

While the long winter signals sleep to some animals, others do not rest. The busy world of the bushy-tailed gray squirrel does not stop, for this animal is active all year. In winter, as well as summer, he cares not only for one nest, but two, three, four, or more. One nest may be an unoccupied hollow of a tree limb; another a large rotted hole once made by a woodpecker. Most often his nest is a skyscraper apartment built high in the treetop. Sometimes this high shelter is mistaken for the nest of a large bird. But unlike bird nests, the squirrel's home has a roof and an entrance on the side.

The squirrel's nest often looks as if it has been carelessly thrown together. Yet his bulky nest of twigs is strong and will provide protection all winter long.

If the squirrel does not seem concerned about neatness, he is concerned about food. Scampering about, he searches the ground for enough nuts to store in his nest. Buried acorns are quickly removed and rushed to his shelter. Again and again he races up and down the tree. And even as the snow starts to fall, the squirrel's never-ending search for food goes on.

Perched on a tree limb, the small English sparrow seems to watch over much of the silent white world below. This is his year-round world, for the English sparrow does not migrate. He can withstand the cold for his high body temperature keeps him warm. But, like other animals, if freezing weather is not his problem, finding food is. The blanket of snow hides any seeds on the ground. So the sparrow furiously scratches through the snow trying to uncover any food. For the sparrow and other resident birds, winter is not easy.

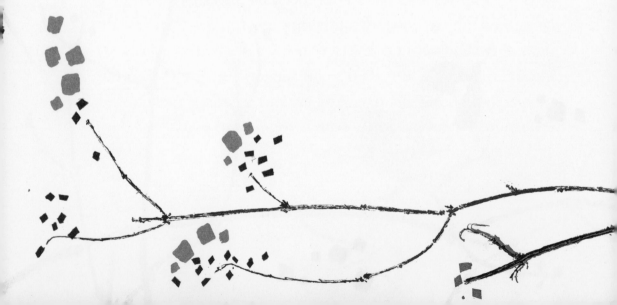

The black-capped chickadee fits well into his black and white winter world. Small and plump, his black cap and bib and his fluffy white and gray body blend into the stark landscape.

Rarely is the chickadee found alone. Flocks of other resident birds are usually nearby. Yet the chickadee easily stands out from among the birds with whom he travels, for the chickadee is a natural acrobat. Often he is seen hanging upside down from a branch or a twig, swinging back and forth. He makes complete turns, flipping head over tail, as he pecks away at a frozen berry. And always, his endless chatter echoes through the wintry silence.

Other resident birds share the winter world of the Northeast. They also share the problem of survival. The nuthatch and the downy woodpecker often join with the chickadee in the search for food. The nuthatch is an upside-down bird. It goes headfirst down a tree trunk searching every inch of bark for hidden insects or their eggs.

Meanwhile, the red patch on the head of the male downy woodpecker moves furiously as he chops into the bark of the tree. He quickly removes any insect larva he finds with his long sticky tongue. Then he continues to peck away until he works his way up the trunk and along the branches.

The large greenish-black starling joins other winter residents in the search for food. Rarely will this happen except in winter. For when warm weather returns the starling often will become an attacker and seize the nests of other birds.

SPRING

Slowly winter passes. The daylight lasts a little longer. The sun seems brighter and a little warmer. The cover of snow begins to melt and patches of earth slowly appear. The air may still be cold, and perhaps a few snowflakes may fall, but winter is near its end. Spring is on its way.

Have you ever thought about the meaning of spring? Spring means to leap, rise suddenly, to awaken, to move forward. And to the world of a tree, spring means a rebirth, a new beginning, a

sudden release, a leap to activity.

The frozen ground begins to thaw. Sap once again flows through the tree. The small reddish buds, bumping out from the branches, seem to swell and within weeks burst forth with green leaves. The fruit, or seed, of the maple soon appears with the leaves, and by late spring the towering maple is clothed in green. The tree, like the world around it, is no longer at rest. It is time to awaken—a time for activity.

The insect world begins to stir. The queen bee takes leave of her resting place. Instinctively, she starts a furious search for a nest. Darting around the tree and along the ground, she explores every hole. Then quickly the queen collects nectar and pollen to store in her new-found nest. Soon she will lay her eggs and remain there until they are hatched.

Other insects awaken with the first signs of spring. And one afternoon, on a calm clear day, thousands of ants from hundreds of nests surrounding the tree swarm into the air. On one day, and one day alone, all the ants in a given colony will sail into the sky to mate. When they return to earth, they will never again fly. The queens will pull off their wings. The males will die after landing. But the eggs of the females will be fertilized. The queens will return to their nests for their lifelong job of laying eggs.

Even the brightly colored garden spider begins to work. She is busily spinning her web in the grass. The slow lumbering movements of two caterpillars tell the world that they too are awake. For the woolly bear and the larvae of the viceroy butterfly, spring has also arrived.

Spring brings the first litter to the female gray squirrel. Her five or six babies are almost helpless when born. For almost two months they will not be able to leave their nest and scamper for themselves along the branches of the tree. If danger is near, the mother squirrel will pick them up and rush them to safety. Like most mothers, the female squirrel has little time to rest. Caring for her babies, as well as finding food for herself, takes up all of her time.

At this time there is another change in the life of the gray squirrel. Many of the dry brown acorns collected and eaten during the fall and winter months are no longer to be found. Her diet must change. She begins to nibble on the buds and flowers of nearby trees. She eats the sap of the maple. Often the hungry squirrel leaves cuttings piled several inches high under the tree.

The sounds of the newborn echo below ground as well as above. Within her long underground tunnel the female chipmunk has given birth to four or five babies. They too must be carefully watched and fed. But they grow quickly and within a month look and behave like their parents. Soon they are ready to peek out of their tunnel and, for the very first time, feel the warm sun and see a bright new world.

Then, all day the chipmunks, young and old, scurry away from home gathering food. They collect berries and seeds with their paws and stuff them into their cheeks. Quickly their cheeks get bigger and bigger as they place the food first on one side and then on the other. Then, when the food is balanced in their mouths, they return to their year-round tunnel. For during the hot summer days ahead, the chipmunk will remain cool and comfortable—eating underground.

Trailing their long naked tails behind them, field mice race through the greening grasses. They run swiftly along the smooth paths which they have cleared to their underground burrows.

The paths seem crowded as more and more mice appear. For every two months another litter has been born. Within two more months, the young will have produced their own litter of six to eleven.

Except for natural controls, the world of a tree would quickly be overrun. Field mice would destroy food needed by other animals. Trees would be killed by the constant gnawing at their trunks.

But this will not happen—for the field mice have many enemies. Birds, snakes, and other animals are always ready to attack. Danger is everywhere. So as the mice dart back and forth, their eyes and ears are alert —alert to any approaching enemy.

A fluttering of wings and a loud trilling song suddenly fill the air. For spring marks the return of the many birds who migrate south to escape the freezing cold weather. Among the first to arrive are the red-breasted robins.

Quickly they search for places to build their nests. Within four or five days their cup-shaped nests in the maple are built. Rough on the outside and smooth within, the nests are built of twigs and mud and lined with soft grass. Soon the females will lay three or four small blue eggs each and the first broods will be born.

Among the new green foliage of the tree, a reddish-brown bird appears. Only its spotted white breast reveals its position as it clings to a low-hanging branch. Suddenly it flies to the highest perch in the tree and begins to sing. Its loud song announces to the world below that the wood thrush has returned home. And his home is probably near the nests he lived in last year and the year before.

The green leaves also frame the brilliant orange and black Baltimore oriole. He has taken possession of a nesting site and now awaits the arrival of the female. His loud whistling warns latecomers to move on and find other places to build their nests.

But one bird who hears his warning is not a latecomer. The starling is a year-round resident. And his shimmering body can swoop gracefully into the air at any minute and attack. The starling—a master of flight and a bird of all seasons—must be watched.

SUMMER

Spring turns to summer and the sun rises higher in the sky. From a cloudless blue backdrop its warm rays gently touch the earth. As they do, the whole living world seems to grow stronger.

The leaves and grasses seem brighter green; the brown branches and twigs become more vivid. In this brighter, more

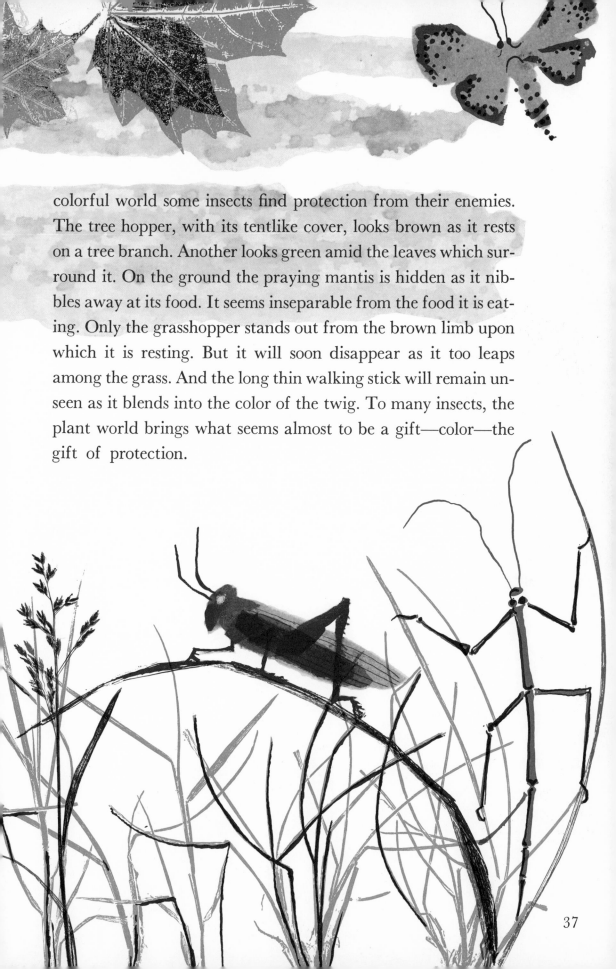

colorful world some insects find protection from their enemies. The tree hopper, with its tentlike cover, looks brown as it rests on a tree branch. Another looks green amid the leaves which surround it. On the ground the praying mantis is hidden as it nibbles away at its food. It seems inseparable from the food it is eating. Only the grasshopper stands out from the brown limb upon which it is resting. But it will soon disappear as it too leaps among the grass. And the long thin walking stick will remain unseen as it blends into the color of the twig. To many insects, the plant world brings what seems almost to be a gift—color—the gift of protection.

If the flourishing plant life hides some insects, it feeds many more. By early summer, plump little aphids begin to appear on the plants. Every few days a new generation is born. Soon their bodies blanket the plant. Then they insert their long sucking mouth parts into the plant and drain off its fluids.

For the black field cricket the whole leaf of a plant provides a meal. Few insects will hold more tightly to their food than the cricket will, while its powerful jaws nibble away. Its appetite is rarely satisfied and it will attack and devour almost anything it can eat.

But in the world of a tree any attacker is soon attacked. For without some control any one species of plant or animal would quickly rule. The larva of the ladybug beetle is one of the controllers. This tiny grayish larva, spotted in red and black, spends its day hunting and attacking the swift-spreading aphids. Within an hour this larva can devour forty or more aphids.

The larva also searches for eggs laid by other insects. Finding a cluster of these eggs, the larva quickly attacks. In a short time it will eat its way from one side of the egg cluster to the other.

Overhead, nestled high on a branch, the brown nest of the robin peeks out from among the green leaves. Lying gently inside the nest are four small robin-blue eggs. These eggs may be the second or even the third brood the female will hatch this year. She will sit on these eggs until they hatch. Her body will keep the eggs warm on cool nights and protect them from the sun during the hot summer's day. She will remain on the eggs while the male sits nearby, ready to protect his family. Then, in thirteen days, small cracks will appear in the eggshells and four baby robins will break their way to freedom.

The newly hatched robins are helpless. No feathers cover their bodies. Their eyes are closed. Their legs are so weak they are unable to stand. They can't feed themselves. Quickly their parents swoop down from the treetop to find food. All day, earthworms are yanked from the ground. Inchworms are plucked from the tree. Soon their beaks are filled and they fly off to the nest where four open mouths wait to be stuffed.

The young fledglings grow quickly. Within two weeks feathers cover their bodies. Their eyes open and their feet grow stronger. They begin to look like their parents.

When they are ready to leave the nest the adult male often takes charge. He feeds them until they are ready to feed themselves. Then slowly they begin to fly. It is not easy. At first they seem afraid. They are awkward and clumsy. But soon they are flying and caring for themselves. As with all animals, another generation begins to live its own life.

Like the fledgling robin, the young gray squirrel is living through his first warm summer. Each new day he has grown. Each new day he has learned. Although only half his adult size, he now cares for his own needs. He scampers from branch to branch and from tree trunk to the ground. He seems more confident about his actions. He gathers his own blackberries from nearby bushes. He darts away at the first hint of danger and cries frantically if a hawk or owl comes near. Through instinct the young squirrel knows how to survive.

By next summer he will be even bigger and stronger. He too will find a mate and start a new generation.

AUTUMN

A slight chill blows across the land. The heat of summer begins to cool. Each day, nighttime appears to arrive a little earlier. The sap which flowed through the maple slows. The green pigment in its leaves appears to fade, and slowly, very slowly, the whole world of the tree starts to change.

A leaf turns red. Another appears streaked with shades of yellow and brown. One by one the leaves take on new brilliance and the tall maple becomes aflame with color. The whole world looks like a giant paint set.

Then a leaf falls. Soon others float and swirl to the ground. Little by little a rainbow of colors lies upon the ground. The leaves dry—then turn brown. Now the tree is almost bare and seems like a giant skeleton stretching for the blue sky. The maple and the world around it seem to prepare for winter.

The young woolly bear scurries downward along a bare branch. It must find shelter before winter arrives. It will crawl under a rock, a piece of wood, or a pile of leaves on the ground. Then, curled up tightly, it will hibernate when the weather turns cold.

Also needing shelter is a young brilliant-orange lady-bug beetle. Its search will lead under the bark of a dead limb where it will rest during the long cold winter. Sometimes, when the winter sun is warm, it will awaken, fly off, and return to finish its sleep.

The garden spider dangles from a silken thread and lowers herself to a branch. There, in a small crevice, she will place a small sac of tiny eggs. Then she will die. The eggs will stay unhatched until spring returns and a new generation of spiders will be born.

For the adult cricket the approaching winter also means death. It has lived its life, and the female prepares for its new generation by laying her eggs beneath the ground.

The fluttering of the viceroy butterfly still can be seen. But soon it too
will disappear. For as autumn turns
colder, the brilliant-colored viceroy
will not survive. Only its young will
live through the late autumn and winter, carefully protected in its shelter of
silk and a rolled-up leaf.

Almost hidden by the quickly
browning grass, the grasshopper
spends its last days of life. Soon it too
will prepare for its new generation.
Like the cricket, the female grasshopper will lay her eggs in the ground. All
winter they will remain below the
freezing winds, and hatch in spring as
tiny models of their parents.

As for wasps, only the fertilized queens will live. But they too must seek shelter before the first freeze. Only the queens, which will hibernate all winter, can produce new colonies in spring.

And of all ways of surviving, none is more unusual than that of honeybees. As cold weather arrives, they will gather together in their hives. Then, like a buzzing golden ball, they will start a furious dance. All this activity will raise the temperature in the hives and prevent the bees from freezing.

The busy life of the gray squirrel will remain busy all through autumn. Unlike most insects, his life is not ended. Unlike some animals, he will not hibernate. In fact, he seems more active now than ever before. As a resident animal he must carefully prepare for winter.

The plump berries he gathered all summer are gone. The sweet sap of the maple has dried. Now he must scurry even more quickly to find new food. He gathers and stores nuts and acorns from the trees, or from the ground where they have dropped. It is easier to find food now than it will be when snow covers the ground. His new fondness for nuts is not a matter of taste. For all winter this food will provide the heat and energy he needs to withstand the cold.

A rustling of dry leaves signals that the field mice are still active. Many different generations are now darting back and forth. And, as each generation is born, housing becomes a problem. The ending of autumn means that many new shelters must be found and stocked with food. They explore deserted tunnels under the ground. They visit nests left by birds who have migrated for warmer climates.

With their large eyes and ears and long whiskers, they carry on the search throughout the night. When shelter is found and stored with seeds, field mice will be able to eat. But even when the snow falls, they will still dart from their tunnels to restock their supply.

The tawny chipmunk is also alert to the coming of winter. He too scampers among the leaves in search of nuts and acorns. Although not an expert climber like the squirrel, the chipmunk will scurry up a tree to get his food.

Then, returning to his underground home, the chipmunk will head for the largest room in his tunnel. There he will store his food under his bed of shredded grasses and leaves. Quickly the bed will rise—higher and higher and higher. When the chipmunk finally retires to his bed in late autumn, he nearly touches the ceiling. But when spring returns he will be almost down to the floor. His winter appetite will lower his bed.

As autumn turns colder and the leaves slowly fall, the migratory birds become more restless. They streak from one branch to another. They fly a short distance and quickly return. Winter is approaching. Food in the Northeast soon will be scarce. Insects will be hidden from view, seeds will be covered with snow, and berries will grow no more. The oriole, the robin, and other migratory birds begin to leave. Their trip will be long and may take many weeks. But they must leave if they are to survive.

Then, as if by some mysterious signal, young and old leave their perches and flock to the sky. From all over the Northeast other birds join them. An umbrella of birds covers the sky as thousands streak south.

But they will not always be gone. When the warm sun of spring returns, these birds will once again return to fill the world of a tree with song.

Winter. The snow falls. Amid this white and peaceful world stands a tall, almost bare maple tree. The tree seems lifeless . . . but it is not.

A native New Yorker, STANLEY KLEIN, author of A WORLD IN A TREE, went to public schools in that city and was graduated from New York University with a degree in both chemistry and history. After a period of time running his own automobile agency, he decided he much preferred to teach school. Accordingly, he spent several years teaching elementary and junior high school students, and then became an instructor at Southern Connecticut State College. It was there that he discovered his love for writing for children, and spent about five years as a writer-editor of a nationally circulated elementary school classroom newspaper. At present, he is a managing editor in a well-known textbook publishing house. He lives in Stamford, Connecticut, with his wife and two young daughters.

MARIAN MORTON, the illustrator of A WORLD IN A TREE, now lives in New York City, where she and her husband—a sculptor—have their own studio. She was born in St. Louis, where she studied at the St. Louis School of Fine Arts, moved to Chicago to study at the Chicago Fine Arts Institute, then moved to New York, where she studied at the Art Students League. For several years, with her husband, she lived in Argentina, Brazil, Mexico, Central America, Spain, France, Italy, and North Carolina. Then the family, which included two children, moved to Mamaroneck, New York, where, in her own back yard, Mrs. Morton found the actual tree that is described and illustrated in this book.